S S I C S

Great American
Short Stories II

O. HENRY

Stories retold by Tony Napoli
Illustrated by James Balkovek

LAKE EDUCATION
Belmont, California

LAKE CLASSICS

Great American Short Stories I

Washington Irving, Nathaniel Hawthorne, Mark Twain, Bret Harte, Edgar Allan Poe, Kate Chopin, Willa Cather, Sarah Orne Jewett, Sherwood Anderson, Charles W. Chesnutt

Great American Short Stories II

Herman Melville, Stephen Crane, Ambrose Bierce, Jack London, Edith Wharton, Charlotte Perkins Gilman, Frank R. Stockton, Hamlin Garland, O. Henry, Richard Harding Davis

Great British and Irish Short Stories

Arthur Conan Doyle, Saki (H. H. Munro), Rudyard Kipling, Katherine Mansfield, Thomas Hardy, E. M. Forster, Robert Louis Stevenson, H. G. Wells, John Galsworthy, James Joyce

Great Short Stories from Around the World

Guy de Maupassant, Anton Chekhov, Leo Tolstoy, Selma Lagerlöf, Alphonse Daudet, Mori Ogwai, Leopoldo Alas, Rabindranath Tagore, Fyodor Dostoevsky, Honoré de Balzac

Cover and Text Designer: Diann Abbott

Library of Congress Catalog Number: 94-075030
ISBN 1-56103-022-8
Printed in the United States of America
1 9 8 7 6 5 4 3 2 1

CONTENTS

🌿 Lake Classic Short Stories 🌿

> *"The universe is made of stories, not atoms."*
> —Muriel Rukeyser

> *"The story's about you."*
> —Horace

Everyone loves a good story. It is hard to think of a friendlier introduction to classic literature. For one thing, short stories are *short*—quick to get into and easy to finish. Of all the literary forms, the short story is the least intimidating and the most approachable.

Great literature is an important part of our human heritage. In the belief that this heritage belongs to everyone, *Lake Classic Short Stories* are adapted for today's readers. Lengthy sentences and paragraphs are shortened. Archaic words are replaced. Modern punctuation and spellings are used. Many of the longer stories are abridged. In all the stories, painstaking care has been taken to preserve the author's unique voice.

Lake Classic Short Stories have something for everyone. The hundreds of stories in the collection cover a broad terrain of themes, story types, and styles. Literary merit was a deciding factor in story selection. But no story was included unless it was as enjoyable as it was instructive. And special priority was given to stories that shine light on the human condition.

Each book in the *Lake Classic Short Stories* is devoted to the work of a single author. Little-known stories of merit are included with famous old favorites. Taken as a whole, the collected authors and stories make up a rich and diverse sampler of the story-teller's art.

Lake Classic Short Stories guarantee a great reading experience. Readers who look for common interests, concerns, and experiences are sure to find them. Readers who bring their own gifts of perception and appreciation to the stories will be doubly rewarded.

O. Henry
(1862–1910)

About the Author

O. Henry was the pen name of William Sydney Porter. He was born in Greensboro, North Carolina, during the Civil War. He worked in his uncle's pharmacy before drifting off to Texas. In Texas, he spent 10 years in various jobs, including that of bank teller. After a romantic elopement, he began writing in his spare time.

Then came the great tragedy of Porter's life. He was accused of embezzling money from the bank where he worked. In a panic, he ran off to Central America. When he heard that his wife was ill, he returned and stayed with her until she died. Only then did he give himself up. He was tried, convicted, and sentenced to five years in prison. For good behavior, he was let out after three years and three months.

There is reason to believe that Porter was innocent all along. The doctor at the prison got to know him well, for Porter worked in the prison pharmacy. He believed Porter when he said, "I never stole a thing in my life. I was sent here for embezzling bank funds—not one cent of which I ever got. Someone else got it all, and I am doing time for it."

Porter got many of his story ideas from other prisoners. He wrote at least 12 stories before he was released. No one knows the exact number, for he used several pen names. Some say he hid his real name because he was ashamed of his prison record. After he left prison, he went to New York, where he continued to write.

O. Henry's stories are famous for their humor and their surprise endings. If you like fun and surprises, you'll be looking for more O. Henry stories after you read these.

The Ransom of Red Chief

Do "get rich quick" schemes usually work out? In this famous story, two bumbling drifters think they have devised the perfect crime. All they want is a fast $2,000. But what they get is much more—and much less—than they bargained for.

"HA! PALEFACE. DO YOU DARE TO ENTER THE CAMP OF RED CHIEF, THE TERROR OF THE PLAINS?"

The Ransom of Red Chief

It looked like a good thing at the time—but wait till I tell you. My pal Bill Driscoll and I had drifted down south to this little town called Summit. It seemed to be a pleasant place, with a lot of good, simple people.

Together, we had about $600. We needed another $2,000 or so to pull off this sweet little land deal up in Illinois. How could we get our hands on that much money? We decided that family ties run strong in a town like Summit. So a kidnapping plan seemed like a good idea. We weren't worried too much about getting caught. Such a small town only had a few lawmen. It should be easy to get away from them and a couple of lazy bloodhounds, we thought.

We decided our victim would be the only child of a well-known citizen named Ebenezer Dorset. The father was rich and well-respected in the town. The kid was a freckle-faced 10-year-old boy with bright red hair. Bill and I figured that the old man would come across with the $2,000 without blinking twice. But wait till I tell you.

Finding a place to stay was easy. In less than an hour we found a nice little cave in a hill behind the town. Once we stored our food there, we were ready to go. That evening after sundown, we rented a buggy and drove it past the Dorset house. We saw the boy playing in the street. He was throwing rocks at a kitten on a neighbor's fence.

Bill called out to him. "Hey, little boy, how would you like to have a bag of candy and take a nice ride?"

The boy didn't answer. What he did do was to throw a rock straight in Bill's eye.

"That will cost the old man an extra $500," Bill grumbled.

The boy put up a fight, but we finally got him in the buggy. We took him back up to the cave to hide out until dark. After dark I drove the buggy back to the stable where we rented it. Then I walked back to our cave on the hillside.

Bill was patching up his wounds. The boy was watching a pot of boiling coffee above the fire near the cave entrance. He had two buzzard tail-feathers stuck in his red hair. When I came in he pointed a stick at me and said, "Ha! Paleface. Do you dare to enter the camp of Red Chief, the terror of the plains?"

"He's all right now," Bill said, looking at all the bruises on his shins. "We're playing Indian, and I'm Old Hank, the Trapper. Red Chief here has captured me and I'm going to be scalped at daybreak. By Geronimo, this kid can kick hard."

Yes, sir, that boy seemed to be having the time of his life. Being up in that cave seemed to make him forget that he was a captive himself. He quickly named me Snake-eye, the Spy. And he announced that when his braves returned from the warpath, I was to be broiled at the stake at sunrise.

In a little while we had supper. The boy stuffed his mouth with bread, bacon, and gravy—and never stopped talking the whole time.

"I like this fine. I never camped out before. I hate to go to school. Rats ate up 16 of Jimmy Talbot's aunt's hen's eggs. Are there any *real* Indians in these woods? I want some more gravy. What makes your nose so red, Hank? My father has lots of money. Are the stars hot? I don't like girls. Have you got any beds to sleep on in this here cave? Why are oranges round?"

We rolled our eyes and looked away. Anything to make him shut up. But the boy kept right on going.

"Does an ox make a noise? Amos Murray has six toes. Why can a parrot talk but a fish can't?"

I think you get the general picture.

Every few minutes he would remember he was pretending to be a pesky Indian. Then he'd let out a war-whoop that made Old Hank the Trapper shiver. That boy had rattled Bill's nerves from the start.

"Red Chief," I said, "would you like to go home?"

"What for?" the kid said. "I don't have any fun at home. I hate to go to school. I like it here. You won't make me go home, will you, Snake-eye?"

"Not right away," I said. "We'll stay here in the cave for a while."

"All *right*," the kid said. "I never had such fun in all my life."

We went to bed around eleven o'clock. We put down some blankets and quilts and put Red Chief between us. He kept us awake for three hours, jumping up and giving out war-whoops. Finally, I fell into a restless sleep. I dreamed I'd been chained to a tree by a mad pirate with red hair.

At daybreak, I was awakened by a series of awful screams from Bill. It's a horrible thing to hear a big, strong man scream his head off in a cave at dawn.

I jumped up to see what all the yelling was about. Red Chief was sitting on Bill's chest. In one hand he had a hunk of Bill's hair. In the other he was holding the sharp knife we used for slicing bacon. He was seriously trying to take Bill's scalp, just as he had promised the night before.

I took the knife away from the kid and made him lie down again. Then Bill calmed himself and lay down on his side of the bed. But he never closed an eye to sleep again as long as the boy was with us. I dozed off for a while. But after some time I remembered what Red Chief had said about burning me at the stake at sunrise. I sat up and leaned against a rock.

"Why are you getting up so soon, Sam?" Bill asked.

"Oh, I got a pain in my shoulder. I thought sitting up would help."

"That's a lie," Bill said. "You was to be burned at sunrise, and you were afraid he'd do it. And he would, too, if he could find a match. Will anybody pay out money to get a kid like that back?"

"Sure," I said. "The kid's just playful, that's all. Now you and the Chief cook up some breakfast. I'm going up to the top of this hill and look around."

I went up on the peak and looked down toward the town. I expected the towns-folk to be searching the countryside for the kidnappers. But everything seemed quiet and peaceful. In fact, it looked as if the whole town was asleep. I thought that perhaps word about the kidnapping hadn't spread yet. So I went back down to have breakfast.

After we ate, the kid took something out of his pocket. It was a piece of leather with strings around it. He walked outside the cave unwinding the strings.

"What's he up to now?" Bill asked. "You don't think he'll run away, do you?"

"Don't worry about it," I said. "You heard what he said. He doesn't have any fun at home. But we've got to work up a plan about the ransom. So far the town doesn't seem too excited about his disappearance. Maybe they haven't realized he's missing yet. His father may think he's at his aunt's house or with one of the neighbors. Tonight we have to send his father a message demanding the $2,000."

Just then we heard another screaming war-whoop. I looked up and saw Red Chief whirling a sling around his head. I ducked, and then heard a thud and a big sigh coming from Bill. A rock the size of a jumbo egg had caught Bill just behind his left ear. He pitched over and fell across the pan of hot water we used for washing the dishes. I dragged him out and poured cold water on his head. It was half an hour before Bill could talk.

"You won't go away and leave me here alone, will you, Sam?" he finally asked.

I didn't answer. I went out and shook that boy until his freckles rattled. "If you don't behave, I'm taking you home," I said. "Are you going to be good?"

"I was only funning," the kid said. "I didn't mean to hurt Old Hank. I'll behave, Snake-eye, as long as you won't send me home. And if you'll let me play the Black Scout today."

"That's for you and Mr. Bill to decide," I said. "I'm going away for a while to take care of some business. Now, you go and apologize for hurting him."

I made the kid and Bill shake hands. Then I took Bill aside and told him I was going over to Poplar Grove. That was a little village a few miles from the cave. I wanted to find out if the people there had heard anything about a kidnapping in Summit.

"You won't leave me alone with him for long, will you, Sam?" Bill whispered.

"I'll be back some time this afternoon," I said. "Keep the boy busy and quiet until I get back. Now let's write the letter to old Dorset."

"I don't think anybody is going to give up $2,000 for that 40-pound, freckled wildcat," Bill said. "But I'm willing to take a chance at $1,500."

I agreed, and we set to writing the letter. We listed our demands. Then we gave Dorset instructions as to how to get in touch with us and where to deliver the ransom. We signed the letter, "Two Desperate Men."

As I was getting ready to leave, the kid came up to me. "Snake-eye, you said I could play the Black Scout while you were gone."

"What kind of a game is it?" I asked.

"I'm the Black Scout," Red Chief said. "I have to ride to the stockade to warn the settlers that the Indians are coming. I'm tired of playing Indian myself. I want to be the Black Scout."

"All right, it sounds harmless to me."

"What do I have to do?" Bill asked.

"You're the horse," Black Scout said. "How can I ride to the stockade without a horse?"

"You better keep him interested till we get the scheme going," I said.

Bill got down on all fours. The look in his eyes was like a rabbit caught in a trap. "How far is it to the stockade, kid?" he said.

"Ninety miles," the kid said as he climbed on Bill's back and dug in his heels.

"Maybe we shouldn't have made the ransom for more than $1,000," Bill groaned. "For Pete's sake, hurry back as fast as you can, Sam."

I walked over to Poplar Grove and sat around the post office. Finally I heard two fellows talking about some trouble in Summit. They said that people were all upset because Ebenezer's boy was either lost or stolen. That was all I needed to know. I mailed the ransom letter and quickly made my way back to the cave.

When I arrived, neither Bill nor the boy were there. I looked around, and even gave out with a yell or two. No answer. So I sat down on some rocks and waited to find out what happened.

In a little while Bill came out from behind some bushes. A few feet behind him was the kid, with a huge grin on his face. Bill stopped, took off his hat, and wiped his face with a handkerchief. The kid stopped about eight feet behind him.

"Sam, I'm sorry, but I couldn't help it. I know I'm a grown man with strong habits of self-defense. But I reached my limit. The boy is gone. I sent him home."

"What was the trouble, Bill?"

"The kid rode me the 90 miles to the stockade. Then when the settlers were rescued, he pretended to feed me 'oats.' Believe me, sand is not a pleasant substitute. Then for an hour I had to explain things to him. 'How come there's nothing in holes? How can a road run both ways? What makes the grass green?' A human can only stand so much, Sam. I took him by the neck and dragged him down the mountain. On the way he kicked my legs black and blue from the knees down.

"But he's gone," Bill continued. "I showed him the road to Summit and shoved him along. I'm sorry we lost the ransom. But it was either that or Bill Driscoll to the madhouse."

Bill was puffing and blowing, but there was a peaceful look on his face.

"Bill, is there any heart disease in your family?" I asked.

"No," he said. "Nothing serious except malaria and accidents."

"Then you might turn around and have a look behind you."

Bill turned around and saw the boy. He turned white and sat down plump on the ground. There he stayed, plucking away at the grass and little sticks. For an hour I was afraid he'd gone crazy. Then I told him that I had a plan to collect the ransom right away. When I said we'd be on our way by midnight, he seemed to feel a little better.

Our letter had told old man Dorset where to leave his reply. The place was a tree near the fence post at the foot of the hill. It was the same place where the ransom was to be left later—if he agreed to our demands. At 8:30 I was up in that tree watching for the messenger with Dorset's answer.

Exactly on time a young boy rode up on a bicycle. He found the box at the foot of the fence post and slipped a piece of paper into it. Then he rode off towards Summit.

I waited an hour to make sure the boy hadn't been followed by the law. Then I hurried back to the cave with the note.

I opened the note, got near a lantern, and read it to Bill. This is what it said:

TWO DESPERATE MEN.
Gentlemen:
I received your letter today in regard to the ransom for the return of my son. I think you are a little high in your demands. I'll make you a counter offer. You bring Johnny home and pay me $250. Then I'll take him off your hands. You'd better come at night. The neighbors believe he is lost. I couldn't be responsible for

*what they would do to anybody they
saw bringing him back.*

With respect,

Ebenezer Dorset

"Great God, what a nerve that man
has!" I screamed out. Then I glanced at
Bill and saw that he had a very strange
look on his face.

"Sam, what's $250 after all?" he asked
quietly. "We've got the money. One more
night of this kid and I'll be ready for a
bed at the crazy house. Actually, I think
old Dorset is making us a generous offer.
You're not going to let the chance go,
are you?"

"Tell you the truth, Bill, this kid has
gotten on my nerves, too," I said. "We'll
give him back, pay the money, and make
our getaway."

We took him home that night. He
agreed to go when we told him his father
had bought him a rifle and moccasins.
And we promised we'd all go out bear
hunting the next day.

It was midnight when we reached Dorset's house. That was just the moment that I should have been taking $1,500 from the box by the fence post. Instead, Bill was counting out $250 and putting it into old Dorset's hand.

When the kid figured out we were going to leave him, he started to scream. He grabbed hold of Bill's leg and held on like a drowning man clings to a life raft. His father had to peel him away gradually, like loose plaster.

"How long can you hold him?" Bill asked in a pleading voice.

"I'm not as strong as I used to be," Dorset said. "But I think I can promise you ten minutes."

"That's enough," Bill said. "In ten minutes I'll be across the southern and central states and halfway to the Canadian border."

Let me tell you. As fat as Bill was, and as good a runner as I am, he was a mile out of Summit before I finally caught up with him.

The Gift
of the Magi

What would you give up for someone you love? This famous love story takes place on Christmas Eve. A poor young wife is desperate to buy a present for her husband. To get it, she decides to sacrifice her most prized possession.

"THE QUEEN OF ENGLAND'S JEWELS WOULD LOSE MUCH
OF THEIR VALUE IF THEIR BEAUTY WERE COMPARED TO
DELLA'S HAIR."

The Gift
of the Magi

One dollar and 87 cents. That was all. And 60 cents of it was in pennies. Pennies that had been saved one and two at a time and only by bulldozing the grocer and the butcher. Her cheeks burned with shame at the cheapness of such close dealings—of penny-pinching. Three times Della counted her money. One dollar and 87 cents was all the money she had. And the next day would be Christmas.

There was clearly nothing left to do but sit down on the shabby little couch and cry. So that's what Della did. And she wondered if life is made up of nothing but sobs, sniffles, and smiles—but mostly sniffles.

While the lady of the house is recovering from her tears—take a look at her home. She lives in a furnished flat that rents for eight dollars a week. In the hallway below is a mailbox so small that no letter could fit inside. Beneath it is a door bell button that doesn't work. Attached to the mailbox is a card bearing the name "Mr. James Dillingham Young." Whenever Mr. Young comes home he is called "Jim" and hugged warmly by his wife—the above-mentioned Della. And this is all very good.

When Della finished her cry, she dried her eyes and powdered her cheeks. Then she stood by the window and sadly looked out at a gray cat walking on a gray fence in a gray backyard. Tomorrow was Christmas Day! And she had only $1.87 to buy a present for Jim. For months she had been saving every penny she could. Yet this was the result.

Of course, 20 dollars a week—Jim's earnings—could only be stretched so far. Household expenses had been greater than she had figured. They always are. Only $1.87 to buy a present for her Jim! She had spent many happy hours planning to buy him a nice gift. It had to be something fine and rare and wonderful—something worthy of the honor of being Jim's wife.

Suddenly Della whirled away from the window and stood before a mirror. Her eyes were shining brightly, but her face had lost its color. Quickly she pulled the clips from her hair and let it fall to its full length.

Now Mr. and Mrs. Young had only two possessions in which they both took great pride. One was Jim's gold watch. It had been his grandfather's and then his father's before him. The other was Della's hair. The Queen of England's jewels would lose much of their value if their beauty were compared to Della's hair. And even King Solomon, counting his riches, would burst with envy at the sight of Jim's beautiful gold watch.

Now Della's hair fell about her, rippling and shining like a waterfall. It reached below her knees and nearly became a piece of clothing for her. Then she quickly piled it up again and pinned it in place. As she did, a tear or two splashed on the worn red carpet.

On went her old brown jacket and her old brown hat. Then, with a whirl of skirts, Della rushed out the door and down the stairs to the street.

She stopped about three blocks away. She was standing in front of a sign that said, "Mrs. Sofronie, Hair Goods of All Kinds." Della took a deep breath and ran up one flight of stairs. When she opened the door, she found herself standing in front of a large, rather cold-looking woman.

"Will you buy my hair?" Della asked in a rush.

"I buy hair," the woman said. "Take your hat off and let's have a look at you."

Down came Della's beautiful hair.

"Twenty dollars," the woman said. She lifted the mass of shiny brown hair with an experienced hand.

"Give it to me quick," Della said.

The next two hours flew by as Della rushed through a dozen stores looking for Jim's present.

At last she found it. Surely it had been made for Jim and no one else. It was a platinum watch chain. The design was simple and clean—its value stated in its substance alone, not in any decoration. Such is the quality of all good things. The watch chain was even worthy of The Watch. As soon as she saw it, she knew that it must be Jim's. It was like him. Simplicity and value—the description applied to both.

The chain cost Della 21 dollars. She hurried home with the 87 cents that she had left over. With that chain on his watch, Jim would never be afraid to check the time in front of anybody. Grand as his watch was, he sometimes looked at it on the sly. She knew it was because of the old leather strap he used in place of a chain.

When Della reached her home, her complete happiness gave way to more practical thoughts. She took out her curling irons and lit the gas on top of the stove. Then she went to work repairing the hair that she had sacrificed for love.

In 30 minutes her whole head was covered with tiny, close-lying curls. She studied herself in the mirror for a long time. She frowned at what she saw and nearly burst into tears.

"Before Jim takes a second look, he'll say I look like some Coney Island dance-hall girl," she said. "But what could I do? Oh, what could I do with a dollar and 87 cents?"

By seven o'clock Della had gotten everything ready. She wanted to put dinner on the moment Jim arrived. He was never late. She doubled the watch chain in her hand and sat on the corner of the table near the door. Suddenly she heard his steps on the stairs below. She turned white for a moment. Then she whispered, "Please, God, make him think that I'm still pretty."

The door opened and Jim stepped in and closed it. She thought he looked thin and serious. He needed a new overcoat and was without gloves.

Jim took just a few steps and then stopped in his tracks. His eyes were fixed on Della. There was a look in his face that she couldn't read, and it frightened her. It was not a look of anger or surprise or horror. His face did not show any of those feelings that she had been prepared for. He simply continued to stare at her with an odd look.

Della got up from the table and went over to him.

"Jim, darling, don't look at me that way," she cried. "I had to sell my hair! I couldn't have lived through Christmas without giving you a nice present. My hair will grow out again—you won't mind, will you? I just *had* to do it. My hair grows awfully fast. Say 'Merry Christmas!,' Jim, and let's be happy! You don't know what a nice—what a beautiful gift I've got for you."

"You've cut off your hair?" Jim asked. He acted as if his mind had not yet accepted what his eyes could plainly see.

"Cut it off and sold it," Della said. "Don't you like me just as well, anyhow? I'm still me without my hair, aren't I?"

Jim looked about the room. He still seemed confused. "You say your hair is gone?" he asked.

"Don't bother to look for it," Della said, trying to sound cheerful. "It's sold and gone. It's Christmas Eve, Jim. Be good to me—for it went for you. Maybe the hairs on my head were numbered," she went on sweetly, "but nobody could ever count my love for you. Shall I put dinner on?"

Suddenly Jim seemed to wake up. He hugged Della for ten seconds. Then he took a package out of his pocket and threw it upon the table.

"Don't make any mistake about me, Dell," he said. "No haircut or shave or shampoo could make me like my girl any less. But when you open that package, you'll see why you had me going for a while at first."

Della's fingers tore at the string and paper. Then she cried out, first in joy, and then in tears and wails a moment later. Jim had to use all of his powers of comforting to get her to stop crying.

For there lay The Combs—the set of combs, side and back—that Della had admired for so long in a Broadway shop window. They were beautiful combs— pure tortoise shell, with jeweled rims. They were just the shade to wear in her beautiful, vanished hair. She knew the combs were expensive. Her heart had yearned for them without any hope of ever owning them. And now they were hers. But the lovely hair they would hold was all gone.

Della hugged the combs to her chest. Then she looked up at her husband with a sad smile. "My hair grows so fast, Jim."

Then she leaped up like a frightened cat and cried, "Oh, oh!"

Jim had not yet seen his beautiful present. She eagerly held it out to him upon her open hand. "Isn't it a dandy, Jim? I hunted all over town to find it. You'll have to look at the time a hundred times a day now. Give me your watch. I want to see how the chain looks on it."

Jim didn't obey her. Instead, he just tumbled down on the couch, put his hands behind his head, and smiled.

"Dell, let's put our Christmas presents away and keep them a while," he said. "They're too nice to use right now. The truth is, I sold the watch to get the money to buy your combs. Now suppose you put dinner on."

The magi, as you know, were the wise men who brought gifts to the Christ child in the manger. They invented the art of giving Christmas presents.

Being wise, their gifts were no doubt wise ones, too. This is a simple story of two foolish young people who unwisely sacrificed for each other the greatest treasures of their house. But here is a final word to the wise of these days: Of all who give and receive gifts, people such as these two are the wisest. Everywhere they are the wisest. They are the magi.

The Last Leaf

In the early 1900's, there were no effective medicines to fight off pneumonia. Without a miracle, the sick young woman in this story may very well die. Her roommate becomes desperate for help. Who would expect that help to come from a strange old man with a special talent?

"OH, I NEVER HEARD OF SUCH NONSENSE!" SUE CRIED.
"WHAT HAVE THOSE OLD IVY LEAVES TO DO WITH YOU
GETTING WELL?"

The Last Leaf

There is a little neighborhood west of Washington Square in New York City. The streets have run crazy here, and broken themselves into small strips called "places." These "places" make strange angles and curves. One street even crosses itself a time or two.

Greenwich Village is the name of this area of New York. Over the years it has become a favorite place for artists to live and work. It is here that our story takes place.

At the top of a three-story brick building, Sue and Johnsy had their studio. "Johnsy" was a nickname for Joanna. One woman was from Maine, the other from California. The two friends had met at an Eighth Street restaurant called Delmonico's. They quickly found that they had a lot in common—including the same tastes in art and food. So they decided to share a studio apartment.

That was in May. In November, a cold, invisible stranger the doctors called *pneumonia* visited the neighborhood. Mr. Pneumonia was not a gentleman. A small woman with blood thinned by California living was not fair game for him. But it was Johnsy he struck down. She lay very still on her bed looking out the windows. All she could see was the blank side of the next brick house.

One morning the busy doctor stopped in to check on Johnsy. Then he told Sue he wanted to talk with her in the hallway. "Your friend has about one chance in ten," the doctor said. "And that chance is for her to *want* to live.

"Right now a lot of people seem to be giving in to pneumonia—as if they're lining up outside the cemetery, waiting to get in," the doctor went on. "It makes the entire field of medicine look helpless. Your friend seems to have made up her mind that she's not going to get well. Does she have anything special on her mind?"

"Sure," Sue said. "She wants to paint the Bay of Naples some day."

"Paint? Nonsense! Has she anything on her mind worth thinking about twice—a man, for example?"

"A man?" Sue said with a harsh laugh. "Is a man worth—but, no, doctor, there is nothing of the kind."

"Well, that's too bad, then," he said. "I will do all that I can—all that science can accomplish. But I worry whenever a patient begins to count the cars in the funeral line. Then I subtract 50 percent from the powers of medicine. Can't you get her interested in something? Try to get her to ask one question about the new winter styles in coats. Then I will promise you a one in five chance, instead of one in ten."

After the doctor left, Sue went into the workroom and had a good cry. Then she walked into Johnsy's room with her head up and chest out. She whistled a happy tune and carried her drawing board with her.

Johnsy lay under the covers with her face toward the window. She hardly made a move. Sue stopped whistling, thinking Johnsy was asleep.

Then Sue began to work. She started a pen-and-ink drawing to illustrate a magazine story.

It's an old story. All young artists must pave their way to Art. Often, they do this by drawing pictures for magazine stories. These are the same stories, of course, that young writers write to find their way to Literature.

As Sue continued to draw, she heard a low sound repeated several times. She quickly went to the bedside.

Johnsy's eyes were open wide. She was looking out the window and counting—counting backward.

"Twelve," she said, and a little later "eleven." Next she counted, "ten," "nine," "eight," and "seven" almost in one breath.

Sue looked out the window. What was there to count? Only a bare, dull yard was visible below. And there was the blank side of the brick building 20 feet away. An old, old ivy vine climbed half way up the brick wall. The cold breath of autumn had taken most of its leaves. Now only the skeleton branches of the vine clung to the crumbling bricks.

"What is it, dear?" Sue asked.

"Six," said Johnsy, in a small whisper. "They're falling faster now. Three days ago there were almost a hundred. It made my head hurt to count them. But now it's easy. There goes another one. There are only five left now."

"Five what, dear?" Sue asked.

"Leaves. On the ivy vine. When the last one falls, I must go, too. I have known that for three days. Didn't the doctor tell you?"

"Oh, I never heard of such nonsense!" Sue cried. "What have those old ivy leaves to do with you getting well? Why, you used to love that vine so! Don't be a silly girl. Just this morning the doctor said that your chances for getting well real soon were—let's see exactly what he said. He said the chances were ten to one!

"Try to take some soup now, and let me go back to my drawing," Sue went on. "Once I finish, I can sell this drawing to the magazine and buy us some groceries."

"You don't have to worry about buying anything for me," Johnsy said. She kept her eyes fixed out the window. "There goes another. No, I don't want any soup. That leaves just four. I want to see that last one fall before it gets dark. Then I'll go, too."

"Johnsy, dear, promise me something, will you?" Sue said. "Keep your eyes closed and don't look out the window until I'm done working. I must hand in these drawings by tomorrow. If I didn't need the light, I'd pull the shade down."

"Couldn't you draw in the other room?" Johnsy asked coldly.

"I'd rather be here by you," said Sue. "Besides, I don't want you to keep looking at those silly ivy leaves."

"Tell me as soon as you have finished," Johnsy said. She closed her eyes and lay as still as a fallen statue. "Because I want to see the last one fall. I'm tired of waiting. I'm tired of thinking. I want to turn loose my hold on everything. Then I could go sailing down, down—just like one of those poor, tired leaves."

"Try to sleep now," Sue said. "I must ask Mr. Behrman to be my model for the old miner. I won't be gone more than a minute. Don't try to move until I come back."

Old Behrman was a painter who lived on the ground floor of their building. He was over 60, and he had a long white beard that curled down from his face. Behrman was a failure in art. For 40 years he had painted without ever having much success. He had always been *about* to paint a masterpiece. But he had never yet begun it. For several years he had painted nothing—except now and then something or other for an advertisement.

Behrman made a little bit of money modeling. He didn't mind posing for the young artists in the neighborhood who couldn't pay for a real model. Behrman had problems. He drank too much, and still talked on and on of his coming masterpiece. Over the years, he had become an angry old man who claimed that softness in anyone was foolish. But he also thought of himself as the protector of the two young women in the studio above.

Sue found Behrman sitting alone in his dark studio. In one corner was a blank canvas on an easel. For 25 years that canvas had been waiting there—for the first stroke of the masterpiece. Sue told him of Johnsy's idea about the leaves. She said she was afraid that Johnsy would simply let go of her hold on the world. In her present mind, Johnsy seemed almost eager to float away like a leaf.

Old Behrman, red eyes flashing, told her what he thought of such ideas.

"Nonsense!" he cried. "Are there such foolish people in the world? People who would die because leaves drop off of a stupid vine! I have never heard of such a thing. No, I will not pose as a model for your fool miner. Why do you allow such silly business to come into her brain? Ah, poor little Miss Johnsy."

"She is very ill and weak," Sue said. "The fever has filled up her mind with strange ideas. I'll go now, Mr. Behrman. If you don't want to pose for me, you don't have to. But I think you are a horrible and strange old man."

"You are just like a woman!" Behrman yelled. "Who said I will not pose? Go on, I will come with you. For half an hour I have been trying to say I am ready to pose. God, no one as good as Miss Johnsy should lie sick in a place like this! Some day I will paint a masterpiece and we shall all go away."

Johnsy was sleeping when they stepped into her room. Sue pulled the shade down to the windowsill. Then she and Behrman went into the next room—where they looked out the window at the ivy vine. Then they looked at each other without speaking. A steady, cold rain was falling. The drizzle was mixed with snow. Behrman, in his old blue shirt, took his seat. He was ready to pose. Sue picked up her board and began drawing.

As soon as she woke up the next morning, Sue quickly went into Johnsy's room. She found her friend staring with dull, wide-open eyes at the drawn green shade.

"Pull it up so I can see," she ordered in a whisper.

Sue did as she was asked. And what a surprise! After a full night of beating rain and strong winds, there remained one ivy leaf that stood out against the brick wall.

It was the last on the vine. The leaf was still dark green near its stem. But its edges were tinted with the yellow of decay. Even in the wind, the little leaf bravely held onto a branch some 20 feet above the ground.

"It is the last one," said Johnsy. "I thought it would surely fall during the night. I heard the wind. I know it will fall today. And I shall die at the same time."

"Dear, dear!" Sue said, leaning her worn face closer to the pillow. "Think of me, if you won't think of yourself. What would I do?"

Johnsy would not answer her. The loneliest thing in the world is a soul when it's getting ready to go on its mysterious, far journey.

Slowly, the day wore away. Just before evening they could still see the lone leaf, clinging to its stem against the wall. Then, when night came, the north wind once again started howling. And the rain beat hard against the windows.

When it was light enough the next morning, Johnsy once again asked her friend to raise the shade.

The ivy leaf was still there.

For a long time, Johnsy lay looking at it. Then she called to Sue, who was heating some chicken soup on the stove.

"I've been a bad girl, Sue," Johnsy said. "Something has made that last leaf stay there—to show me how bad I was. It is a sin to want to die. Please bring me a little soup now, and some milk. No, bring me a hand mirror first. Then pack some pillows around me. I'll sit up and watch you cook."

An hour later she said, "Sue, some day I hope to paint the Bay of Naples."

The doctor came in the afternoon. Once again he spoke with Sue out in the hallway.

"Even chances," he said. "With good nursing, you'll win. And now I must see another case that I have downstairs. Behrman, his name is. He has pneumonia, too. But he is a weak old man. And the attack is bad. There's no hope for him. He goes to the hospital today. He'll be more comfortable there."

The next day the doctor came back. "She's out of danger," he said to Sue. "You've won. The right foods and care will bring her back now—that's all she needs."

That afternoon Sue came to the bed where Johnsy lay. She put one arm around her friend, pillows and all.

"I have something to tell you, Johnsy," she said to her. "Mr. Behrman died of pneumonia today. He was in the hospital. He was ill only two days. On the morning of the first day, the janitor found him in his room downstairs. His shoes and clothing were wet through and icy cold. He couldn't imagine where Mr. Behrman had been on such an awful night.

"Then they found a lantern, still lighted. Beside it was a ladder that had been dragged from its place. They also found some brushes and a palette with green and yellow colors mixed on it. Look out the window, dear—at the last ivy leaf on the wall. Didn't you wonder why it never even moved at all when the wind blew? Ah, dear, it's Behrman's masterpiece. He painted it there the night the last leaf fell."

A Retrieved Reformation

What might happen when a career criminal tries to go straight? In this humorous tale, a former safe-cracker starts life all over again in a small town. Then a twist of fate forces him to make a choice that could send him back to prison.

"ME?" SAID JIMMY IN HIS BEST INNOCENT VOICE. "WHY, WARDEN! I NEVER WAS IN SPRINGFIELD IN MY LIFE!"

A Retrieved Reformation

A guard came to the prison shoe shop to see Jimmy Valentine. When he got there, Jimmy was hard at work stitching uppers. The guard took him to the front office, where the warden handed Jimmy his pardon. It had been signed that morning by the governor.

Jimmy took the pardon in a tired kind of way. He had served nearly ten months of a four-year sentence. He had expected to stay only about three months—at the longest. Jimmy had a lot of friends on the "outside." When a man like that is sent to prison, it is hardly worthwhile to cut his hair.

"Now, Valentine, you'll go out in the morning," the warden said. "Get your life together this time, make a man of yourself. You're not a bad fellow at heart. Stop cracking safes and live straight."

"Me?" Jimmy said in surprise. "Why, I never cracked a safe in my life."

"Oh, no, of course not," the warden laughed. "Let's see now. How was it that you happened to get sent up on that Springfield job? Was it because you wouldn't prove an alibi? Were you afraid of embarrassing some high society person? Or was it simply a case of a mean old jury that had it in for you? It's always one or the other with you innocent victims."

"Me?" said Jimmy in his best innocent voice. "Why, warden! I never was in Springfield in my life!"

"Take him back, Cronin," the warden said with a smile. "Fix him up with some outgoing clothes. Unlock him at seven in the morning and bring him to the bullpen. And you, Valentine—you'd better think over my advice."

At 7:15 the next morning Jimmy was in the warden's outer office. He had on a poorly fitted suit and a pair of stiff, squeaky shoes. They were the same kind of cheap clothes the state hands out to all its former "guests."

The clerk handed Jimmy a train ticket and a five-dollar bill. With that small handout, the law expected him to get on the straight road and become a good citizen. The warden shook his hand. Valentine, #9762, was placed on the books as "Pardoned by Governor." And Mr. James Valentine walked out into the sunshine.

Jimmy paid no attention to the song of the birds or the smell of the flowers. He headed straight for a restaurant. There he tasted the first sweet joys of freedom in the form of a broiled chicken and a glass of wine. After dinner, he took his time walking to the station and boarding his train. Three hours later he got off at a small town near the state line. He went to Mike Dolan's cafe and found Mike alone behind the bar.

"Sorry we couldn't make it sooner, Jimmy, me boy," Mike said. "But we had that protest from Springfield to fight. The governor nearly changed his mind. Are you feeling all right?"

"Fine," Jimmy said. "Got my key?"

With his key in hand, Jimmy went up to his room. Everything was just as he had left it. Ben Price's collar button was still on the floor. It had been torn from the police officer's shirt the night that Jimmy was arrested.

Jimmy pulled down a folding bed from the wall. Then, from behind a wall panel, he pulled out a dusty suitcase. He opened it and looked proudly at the best set of burglar's tools in the East. It was a full set, made of special steel. All the latest designs in drills, punches, bits, and clamps were right there in front of him. And there were two or three special tools invented by Jimmy himself. It had cost more than $900 to have the set made— at a place that handled special orders for guys like Jimmy.

In half an hour Jimmy walked back downstairs and through the cafe. Now he was dressed in tasteful and well-fitted clothes. And he was carrying his dusted and cleaned suitcase.

"Anything going on?" Mike Dolan asked in a friendly manner.

"Me?" Jimmy said in a puzzled tone. "I don't understand. I'm working for the New York Short Snap Biscuit Cracker and Wheat Company."

This statement delighted Mike so much that he offered Jimmy a seltzer-and-milk drink on the spot. Mike knew that Jimmy never touched "hard" drinks.

A week after Jimmy's release, a neat job of safe burglary was pulled in Richmond, Indiana. There were no clues as to who did the job. Only $800 was taken. Then two weeks later a "burglar-proof" safe in Logansport was played to the tune of $1,500. Now the police began to get interested.

Next an old-fashioned bank safe in Jefferson City was hit for $5,000. The losses were now high enough to bring the matter to Ben Price's attention. When the police compared their notes, it became clear that the same methods were used in each burglary. Ben Price investigated the scenes of the robberies.

"This is Dandy Jim Valentine's work," Price said later. "He's back in business. Look at the knob on that combination lock. It was jerked out as easy as you could pull up a radish in wet weather! Valentine's got the only clamps that can do a job like that. And look how clean those tumblers were punched out! Jimmy always has to drill just one hole. Yes, I guess Mr. Valentine is the man I want. Next time he'll serve his bit without any early release from some governor's pardon."

Ben Price knew Jimmy's habits. He had learned them while working up the Springfield case. Jimmy liked quick get-aways, no partners, and the company of high society. These careful habits had helped Mr. Valentine become a successful criminal. Soon the news was out that Ben Price was once again on Jimmy's trail. That made other people with burglar-proof safes feel a little more at ease.

One afternoon Jimmy Valentine and his suitcase climbed down off a train in Elmore. Now, Elmore was a little town in Arkansas—just five miles off the main highway. As he always did, Jimmy walked casually through town toward the hotel. He looked like an athletic young senior just home from college. No one could have guessed who he was or what he was doing there.

Jimmy stopped to stare as a young lady crossed the street and passed him at the corner. As she entered the Elmore Bank, something strange happened. Jimmy looked into her eyes—forgot what he was—and somehow became another man. She lowered her eyes and blushed slightly. Young men of Jimmy's style and good looks were rare in Elmore.

Jimmy walked over to a boy who was loafing on the steps of the bank as if he owned it. To pass the time, Jimmy began to ask the boy questions about the town. As they talked, Jimmy fed the boy dimes every few minutes. Before long the young lady came out of the bank. She seemed totally unaware of the handsome young man with the suitcase. She went on her way without so much as a glance at him.

"Isn't that Miss Polly Simpson?" Jimmy asked the boy.

"Naw," said the boy. "She's Annabel Adams. Her pa owns the bank. What did you come to Elmore for? Is that a gold watch chain? I'm going to get a bulldog. Got any more dimes?"

Jimmy turned away from the boy and walked over to the Planters' Hotel. There he registered as Ralph D. Spencer and then struck up a conversation with the desk clerk. Jimmy told him he was thinking about starting up a business in Elmore. How was the shoe business in town? Was there an opening?

The clerk was very friendly. Yes, chances should be good in the shoe line, he said. There wasn't even one shoe store in the town. The dry goods and general stores carried only a few shoes. Business in all lines was fairly good.

Jimmy—that is to say, Mr. Spencer—told the clerk he thought he'd stay in town a few days and take a closer look.

The new man, Ralph Spencer, seemed to have arisen from the "ashes" of the old Jimmy Valentine. These were ashes left by the flame of a sudden and unexpected attack of love. As it happened, Ralph Spencer stayed in Elmore and did well. He opened a shoe store and built up a good run of trade.

Socially, he was also a success. He made many friends. And he accomplished the wish of his heart—he met Miss Annabel Adams. After a year, they were engaged to be married. Before long Jimmy had won the respect of the community, and more importantly—Annabel's father.

Then one day Jimmy sat down in his room and wrote the following letter. He mailed it to the safe address of one of his old friends in St. Louis.

DEAR OLD PAL,

I want you to be at Sullivan's place in Little Rock next Wednesday night at 9:00. I want you to wind up some matters for me. And I want to make you a present of my tools. Say, Billy, I quit the old business a year ago. Now I've got a nice store. I'm making an honest living. And I'm going to marry the finest girl on earth two weeks from now. After I get married, I'm going to sell out and go West. Out there I won't be in much danger of having old scores brought up against me. Be sure to be at Sully's, for I must see you. I'll bring along the tools.

Your old friend,
JIMMY

On the Monday night after Jimmy wrote this letter, Ben Price arrived in

Elmore. He walked around town in his quiet way until he learned what he wanted to know. Then he stood outside a drugstore across from Spencer's shoe store. From there he got a good look at Ralph D. Spencer.

"Going to marry the banker's daughter, are you, Jimmy?" he said to himself. "Well, I don't know!"

The next morning Jimmy had breakfast with Annabel's parents. He planned to go to Little Rock that day. He wanted to order his wedding suit and buy a present for Annabel.

After breakfast, the entire Adams family went downtown. Everyone went along—Mr. Adams, Annabel, Jimmy, and Annabel's married sister with her two little girls, ages five and nine. Together, they strolled over to the hotel where Jimmy still lived. He ran up to his room and picked up his suitcase. Then everybody walked over to the bank.

Inside, Jimmy put his suitcase down. Annabel was in a playful, teasing mood.

She put on Jimmy's hat and picked up the suitcase. "My! Ralph, how heavy your bag is. It feels like it's full of gold bricks."

"There's a lot of nickel-plated shoe-horns in there," Jimmy laughed. "I'm going to return them. I thought I'd save some money by taking them to Little Rock."

The Elmore Bank had just put in a new safe and vault. Mr. Adams was very proud of it. He insisted that every-one admire it. Jimmy noticed that the vault was a small one, but it had a special door. The door closed with three solid steel bolts thrown at the same time by a single handle. It also had a time-lock. Mr. Adams proudly explained its workings to Ralph, who only seemed mildly interested. The two children, May and Agatha, were thrilled by the shining metal vault and its funny clock and knobs.

While everyone was looking at the vault, Ben Price wandered in. He stood over by a counter and quietly watched what was going on.

Suddenly there was a scream from the women. While no one was looking, 9-year-old May had accidentally shut Agatha in the vault. And that wasn't the worst of it. She had also shut the bolts and turned the combination knob—as she'd seen Mr. Adams do.

The old banker reached for the handle and tugged at it. "The door *can't* be opened," he groaned. "The clock hasn't been wound. The combination hasn't been set."

Agatha's mother screamed again.

"Quiet!" Mr. Adams shouted. "Agatha, listen to me." In the silence they could hear the muffled cries of the panicked child inside the vault.

"There isn't a man closer than Little Rock who can open that door," Mr. Adams said. "My God, Spencer, what shall we do? That child can't breathe for long in there. There isn't enough air—and she could die from fright!"

Annabel turned to Jimmy. "Can't you do something, Ralph?" she begged. "*Try*, won't you!"

Jimmy looked at her with an odd, soft smile on his lips and in his eyes. "Annabel, give me that rose you're wearing," he said.

Annabel could hardly believe her ears. But she took the rose from her shoulder and placed it in his hand. Jimmy stuffed it into his vest pocket. Then he threw off his coat and rolled up his shirt sleeves. And with that act Ralph D. Spencer passed away and Jimmy Valentine took his place.

"Everyone get away from the door," Jimmy ordered.

He set his suitcase on the table and opened it up. From that moment on, he seemed unaware of anyone else. He laid out the shining, odd tools and worked swiftly, whistling as he did. The others watched him as if they were under a spell.

In a minute, Jimmy's favorite drill was biting smoothly into the steel door. In ten minutes—breaking his own record—he threw back the bolts and opened the door.

Agatha ran out and was gathered into her mother's arms.

Jimmy Valentine put on his coat and walked towards the front door. As he went, he thought he heard a far-away voice that he once knew. He heard the voice call, "Ralph!" but he never stopped walking.

At the door a big man stood in his way.

"Hello, Ben!" Jimmy said, still wearing his strange smile. "Come around at last, have you? Well, let's go. I don't know that it makes much difference now."

Then Ben Price acted rather strangely. "Guess you're mistaken, Mr. Spencer," he said. "I don't believe I recognize you. Your buggy's waiting for you, isn't it?"

And with that, Ben Price strolled out the door and down the street.

Thinking About
the Stories

The Ransom of Red Chief

1. All stories fit into one or more categories. Is this story serious or funny? Would you call it an adventure, a love story, or a mystery? Is it a character study? Or is it simply a picture the author has painted of a certain time and place? Explain your thinking.

2. The plot is the series of events that takes place in a story. Usually, story events are linked in some way. Can you name an event in this story that was the cause of a later event?

3. Imagine that you have been asked to write a short review of this story. In one or two sentences, tell what the story is about and why someone would enjoy reading it.

The Gift of the Magi

1. Interesting story plots often have unexpected twists and turns. What surprises did you find in this story?

2. Suppose this story had a completely different outcome. Can you think of another effective ending for this story?

3. Which character in this story do you most admire? Why? Which character do you like the least?

The Last Leaf

1. Look back at the illustration that introduces this story. What character or characters are pictured? What is happening in the scene? What clues does the picture give you about the time and place of the story?

2. Are there friends or enemies in this story? Who are they? What forces do you think keep the friends together and the enemies apart?

3. Good writing always has an effect on the reader. How did you feel when you finished reading this story? Were you surprised, horrified, amused, sad, touched, or inspired? What elements in the story made you feel that way?

A Retrieved Reformation

1. Who is the main character in this story? Who are one or two of the minor characters? Describe each of these characters in one or two sentences.

2. Suppose that this story was the first chapter in a book of many chapters. What would happen next?

3. Interesting story plots often have unexpected twists and turns. What surprises did you find in this story?

Thinking About the Book

1. Choose your favorite illustration in this book. Use this picture as a springboard to write a new story. Give the characters different names. Begin your story with something they are saying or thinking.

2. Compare the stories in this book. Which was the most interesting? Why? In what ways were they alike? In what ways different?

3. Good writers usually write about what they know best. If you wrote a story, what kind of characters would you create? What would be the setting?